Mike Servello has once agai[n]
God upon his life and minis[try]
Mike has tapped into the tru[th]
tion to flow though the church to society, to our cities and our
nations. Some people write about what they see as potential,
a vision to be realized. Mike writes from the standpoint of the
vision fulfilled; it has been brought to reality. He is a model for
all believers who desire to reach a lost and confused world.
Read it, get convicted and live out the vision.

Frank Damazio
Senior Pastor, City Bible Church, Portland, Oregon

In *Reach of the Cross*, Pastor Mike Servello skillfully applies
the potent effects of Jesus' death on the cross to five contempo-
rary realms of human experience-Government and Politics; Race
Relations; Business and Finance; Social Problems; and Spiritual
Warfare for Souls. Using five notable Bible characters, Pastor
Mike demonstrates, both theologically and practically, how to
apply the powerful principles of the cross of Christ to daily pro-
fessional circumstances. This book shows believers just how far
the victorious, overcoming domain of the risen Christ reaches
into "real-life" experience. This is a "must read" for pastors,
leaders and those on the front lines in the marketplace.

Wendell Smith
Senior Pastor, City Church of Seattle

I just read Mike Servello's manuscript of his book, *Reach of the
Cross*. This classic book on the redemption and the power of the
cross will be a blessing to both believers and non-believers.
It is power-packed with principles that will enable the
reader to embrace the cross of Jesus Christ for its full and complete deliverance for body, mind soul and spirit.
It is written in simplicity and clarity and not in a theo-
logical dissertation. It will bless both young and old, both schol-
ar and student. I highly recommend this book!

Apostle Emanuele Cannistraci
Prophet, Teacher, Evangelist, Missionary

Dedicated to the church family at

Mt. Zion Ministries in Utica, NY.

Thank you for your faithfulness in standing

with us through the years.

REACH
OF
THE
CROSS

PASTOR MIKE SERVELLO

Mt Zion Ministries

931 Herkimer Road
Utica, New York 13502
www.mzm.org

Mt Zion Ministries is a local church with a vision to reach the world. We are a non-denominational Christian church that believes the Bible is the Word of God. We are here to teach people how to live a better life by getting help from the One who gave us life.

Reach of the Cross

ISBN 0-9740572-4-X

Published by *Life*Truth *a division of*
DS*Lisi* *Inc.*
8271 Rt. 274, PO Box 171, Holland Patent, NY 13354 www.lifestruth.com

Editing: Beth Clark, Mike Hughes, Marianne Lange, Kim Lisi
Cover and Interior Design: Stephen Lisi

CONTENTS

FOREWORD

There is no greater message or truth that has affected mankind than the cross of Christ. Just the thought of all mankind without this world-changing event defies our imagination.

It is the "cross" that has determined natural blessing or poverty in many nations. We have nothing to brag about – only our humble realization that if it wasn't for the accomplishment of the cross, where would our world be.

Mike focuses on what really took place as a result of one man taking on the sin and rebellion of the whole world. No portion of our society was left out. Our Lord took all that is bad and corrupt and exchanged it for all that is good and pure.

I have known Mike and Barbara Servello for over two decades and I see in them, their church and their city, the fruit of the cross. What a wonderful example to see civil government, social issues, poverty, race issues and I could go on and on, affected by the benefits of the cross. The cross will touch the lowest and the highest, the rich and the poor, the educated and uneducated. Jesus makes the difference through the great exchange!

DICK IVERSON
founded Bible Temple, now City Bible Church, Portland, Oregon and Chairman of Ministers Fellowship International

INTRODUCTION

In the twenty-first century, the entire world seems to be in turmoil. In many nations there are forces working constantly to remove any mention of God and the influence of Christianity from public life. As the Word of God and morality are removed, we are being plunged into greater and greater confusion and distress.

What we desperately need today is revival - a worldwide, earthshaking move of the Holy Spirit drawing people to repentance and salvation. This same cry has gone up before God through the ages. The ancient words of Psalm 85:6 say, "Won't you revive us again, so your people can rejoice in you?" (NLT). True revival results in people who return wholeheartedly to the Lord and forsake their sins and ungodly lifestyles. When people's hearts change, everything changes! Desires change, priorities change, choices of entertainment change, interests change, spending habits change, business practices change - all things become new!

Revival means hearts transformed, lives changed, marriages and families restored – a new beginning! We often stop short. We are content to be born again and then sit quietly in church waiting for Jesus to return. That was never God's plan for us. Our faith should impact our world! We must take the gospel out of the church and bring it back into the streets where people desperately need hope. Remember - Jesus was not crucified in a church, but in the marketplace for all to see.

Revival will lead to reformation and community transformation. Reformation begins when Christians live out their faith in practical ways. We should be involved in bettering our communities. Christians should be an influence in education, politics, legislation, social programs, helping the poor and in every other sphere where God has given them influence. God changes people and people change communities.

The time for action is now; we must get involved and press on. It is time for us to echo the words of the prophet Habakkuk and cry out, "I have heard all about you, Lord, and I am filled with awe by the amazing things you have done. In this time of our deep need, begin again to help us, as you did in years gone by. Show us your power to save us. And in your anger, remember your mercy" (Habakkuk 3:2, NLT).

Indeed, God has the power to save us and He sent

Jesus into the world to identify with us and to die on the cross for us. In this book, you will read about five of the people who were present when Jesus was crucified. I believe these individuals represent five specific areas of modern-day society and present us with a powerful prophetic picture of five areas in our world today where God desires to bring change. As we look at Jesus' impact on these people, we see how His work on the cross can reach into various areas of our world today and make a significant difference.

As believers whose lives have been radically impacted and changed by the work of the cross, we need to comprehend the reach of the cross - the power of the cross, the power of the love of God, and the power of salvation - that extends to a world desperate for change. Jesus wants to reach into our world with love and passion, but seemingly, the world does not understand this. Many people suppose they can bypass the cross and create their own way to God. They think the message of the cross is foolishness, as the apostle Paul observed in 1 Corinthians 1:18, "I know very well how foolish the message of the cross sounds to those who are on the road to destruction. But we who are being saved recognize this message as the very power of God" (NLT).

The Cross may indeed sound foolish to people

11

who are on their way to destruction, but once they
open their hearts and experience the love of God,
they realize the cross is the power of God to salvation! Scripture affirms, "I will destroy human wisdom
and discard the most brilliant ideas" (1 Corinthians
1:19). Never forget that "salvation belongs to the
Lord" (Psalm 3:8). Salvation does not come from
man; it is not man's way; it is not man's plan; it is
not man's method. Salvation belongs to the Lord. It
is God's plan, God's way. He alone is the Author of
our salvation.

When we accept God's way of salvation provided
by Jesus' sacrifice on the cross, we receive the very
blessing of God upon our lives. As the awesome
power of the cross reaches into society, God's blessing
will also be upon our cities and our nations, and it
will bring vibrant transformation to the world.

CHAPTER 1

THE GREAT EXCHANGE

Seven hundred years before Jesus' crucifixion, the prophet Isaiah got a glimpse of the cross and wrote a powerful and graphic account of it. Isaiah says Jesus willingly gave His life and was treated as a criminal. He carried the sins of the people and asked forgiveness of those who had sinned, "...He poured out His soul unto death, and He was numbered with the transgressors, and He bore the sin of many, and made intercession for the transgressors" (Isaiah 53:12).

Since the beginning of time one of the deepest desires in human hearts has been for forgiveness. Is it possible that the deep stains of sin in the soul could be forgiven and cleansed? In Psalm 25:16-20, David describes the condition of someone trapped by sin and the feelings of helplessness it produces, "Come, Lord, and show me your mercy, for I am helpless, overwhelmed, in deep distress; my problems go from bad to worse. Oh, save me from them all! See my sorrows; feel my pain; forgive my sins. See how many enemies I have and how viciously they hate me! Save me from them! Deliver my life from their power! Oh, let it never be said that I trusted you in vain!" (TLB).

In the Old Testament God gave His people instructions about how to deal with their sins. He required them to assemble before Him once a year for a time of national forgiveness and cleansing. This day was called the Day of Atonement because on that day their sins would be atoned for or covered.

This atonement began with two goats that had been brought to the temple. The High Priest would slay one goat and sprinkle its blood as a covering for the sins of the people. Leviticus 16:15, 16 explains this, "Then Aaron must slaughter the goat as a sin offering for the people and bring its blood behind the inner curtain. There he will sprinkle the blood on the atonement cover and against the front of the Ark, just as he did with the bull's blood. In this way, he will make atonement for the Most Holy Place, and he will do the same for the entire Tabernacle, because of the defiling sin and rebellion of the Israelites" (NLT).

The High Priest would then lay his hands on the head of the second living goat and confess over that animal the sins of the nation. This goat, called a "scapegoat," was then to be released in the wilderness. This represented the removal of the sin and guilt of the nation as the goat "bore" the people's offenses in its body and symbolically took them away. We read about this in Leviticus 16:21, 22 which says, "He is to lay both of his hands on the goat's head and confess over it all the sins and rebellion of the Israelites. In this way, he will lay the people's sins on the head of the goat; then he will send it out into the wilderness, led by a man chosen for this task. After the man sets it free in the wilderness, the goat will carry all the people's sins upon itself into a desolate land" (NLT).

Hebrews 10:4 teaches us that, ". . . it is not possible for the blood of bulls and goats to take away sins" (NLT). Though this verse is from the New Testament, the people in Old Testament days certainly understood that this ceremony only covered their sins, and looked forward to the day when God would no longer cover their sins, but remove them completely and permanently.

For sin to be removed forever, people need a Savior, a substitute. Animals could never be a proper substitute because they are not of the same nature as humans; they cannot identify with us. Besides that, I am sure that no animal knowingly and willingly gave itself as a sacrifice to atone for the sins of others. But we know that Jesus became man, just like you and me, to totally identify with us in everything we experience. Jesus also willingly laid His life down as a substitute for us. He took our punishment; He paid the full price for our sins. He became both the sacrificial lamb that was slain, whose innocent blood was shed to forgive our sins, and the scapegoat who took all our sins into Himself and carried them away.

Hebrews 9:12 reminds us of this truth, "Once for all time he took blood into that Most Holy Place, but not the blood of goats and calves. He took his own blood, and with it he secured our salvation forever" (NLT); 2 Corinthians 5:21 further affirms the power of this great exchange, "For God took the sinless Christ and poured into him our sins. Then, in exchange, he poured God's goodness into us!" (LB). What a transaction!

When we think about the passion of Jesus and the reach of the cross, we must realize that the power of the cross is not limited to our salvation alone. The power of the cross, the power of the love of God, and the power of salvation can reach into our world and make a difference.

CHAPTER 2

THE FIVE AT THE CROSS

I want to highlight five people who were forever changed as Jesus journeyed to Calvary. Each had their own significant encounter with Him. I describe the results of their experiences as the "reach of the cross."

In Mark 15:6-47, the Bible tells us that the cross reached to Barabbas; it reached to Simon of Cyrene, it reached to Joseph of Arimathea; it reached to a criminal crucified next to Jesus; and it reached to a Roman centurion. Each person presents a prophetic picture of what God wants to do in our world today.

Read this story with me and pay attention to these five people whose lives were so radically impacted by Jesus' crucifixion:

It was the governor's custom to release one prisoner each year at Passover time - anyone the people requested. One of the prisoners at that time was Barabbas, convicted along with others for murder during an insurrection. The mob began to crowd in toward Pilate, asking him to release a prisoner as usual. "Should I give you the King of the Jews?" Pilate asked. (For he realized by now that the leading priests had arrested Jesus out of envy.) But at this point the leading priests stirred up the mob to demand the release of Barabbas instead of Jesus. "But if I release Barabbas," Pilate asked them, "what should I do with this man you call the King of the Jews?" They shouted back, "Crucify him!" "Why?" Pilate demanded. "What crime has he committed?" But the crowd only roared the louder, "Crucify him!" So Pilate, anxious to please the crowd, released Barabbas to them. He ordered Jesus flogged with a lead-tipped whip, then turned him over to the Roman soldiers to crucify him. The soldiers took him into their headquarters and called out the entire battalion. They dressed him in a purple robe and made a crown of long, sharp thorns and put it on his head. Then they saluted, yelling, "Hail! King of the Jews!"

They beat him on the head with a stick, spit on him, and dropped to their knees in mock worship. When they were finally tired of mocking him, they took off the purple robe and put his own clothes on him again. Then they led him away to be crucified. A man named Simon, who was from Cyrene, was coming in from the country just then, and they forced him to carry Jesus' cross. (Simon is the father of Alexander and Rufus.) And they brought Jesus to a place called Golgotha (which means Skull Hill). They offered him wine drugged with myrrh, but he refused it. Then they nailed him to the Cross. They gambled for his clothes, throwing dice to decide who would get them. It was nine o'clock in the morning when the crucifixion took place. A signboard was fastened to the Cross above Jesus' head, announcing the charge against him. It read: "The King of the Jews." Two criminals were crucified with him, their crosses on either side of his. And the people passing by shouted abuse, shaking their heads in mockery. "Ha! Look at you now!" they yelled at him. "You can destroy the Temple and rebuild it in three days, can you? Well then, save yourself and come down from the Cross!"

The leading priests and teachers of religious law also mocked Jesus. "He saved others," they scoffed, "but he can't save himself! Let this Messiah, this king of Israel, come down from the Cross so we can see it and believe him!" Even the two criminals who were being crucified with Jesus ridiculed him. At noon, darkness fell across the whole land until three o'clock. Then, at that time Jesus called out with a loud voice, "Eloi, Eloi, lema sabachthani?" which means, "My God, my God, why have you forsaken me?" Some of the bystanders misunderstood and thought he was calling for the prophet Elijah. One of them ran and filled a sponge with sour wine, holding it up to him on a stick so he could drink. "Leave him alone. Let's see whether Elijah will come and take him down!" he said. Then Jesus uttered another loud cry and breathed his last. And the curtain in the Temple was torn in two, from top to bottom. When the Roman officer who stood facing him saw how he had died, he exclaimed, "Truly, this was the Son of God!" Some women were there, watching from a distance, including Mary Magdalene, Mary (the mother of James the younger and of Joseph), and Salome. They had been followers of Jesus and had cared for him while he was in Galilee. Then they and many other women had come with him to Jerusalem. This all happened on Friday, the day of preparation, the day before the Sabbath. As evening approached, an honored member of the high council, Joseph from Arimathea (who was waiting for the kingdom of God to come), gathered his courage and went to Pilate to ask for Jesus' body. Pilate couldn't believe that Jesus was already dead, so he called for the Roman military officer in charge and asked him. The officer confirmed the fact, and Pilate told Joseph he could have the body. Joseph bought a long sheet of linen cloth, and taking Jesus' body down from the Cross, he wrapped it in the cloth and laid it in a tomb that had been carved out of the rock. Then he rolled a stone in front of the entrance. Mary Magdalene and Mary the mother of Joseph saw where Jesus' body was laid (Mark 15:6-47, NLT).

This ancient and riveting account of Jesus' death is powerful indeed. And yet, the cross still speaks just as powerfully today. But how does the world respond to it? Oswald Chambers made an interesting observation, "All heaven is interested in the cross of Christ, all hell terribly afraid of it, while men are the only beings who more or less ignore its meaning." In other words, heaven reveres the cross and hell trembles at it while most human beings still have not made up their minds about it!

Let's see how five people in Jesus' day responded to the reach of the cross and as we observe them; let's consider how the power of the cross can touch and change various elements of our society today.

CHAPTER 3

BARABBAS:

THE CROSS REACHES INTO GOVERNMENT AND POLITICS

I believe Barabbas is a prophetic picture of politicians and government leaders who desire to change their world. This hated criminal and zealous revolutionary had committed murder in a plot to overthrow the Roman government and set his people free from Roman oppression. He was also the first person to be set free by Jesus as the journey to Calvary begins.

Things had not gone as planned for Barabbas. I wonder if he thought about how all this had happened to him as he awaited judgment in his dark prison cell. He must have asked himself: How did I end up in a place like this? How did my desire for freedom lead to murder and now to my own certain execution? Is it possible, in the damp darkness of his surroundings, that he cried out to God asking for mercy, asking for another chance, for a fresh start, wishing to be a free man again?

We are not likely to ever find out exactly what took place in Barabbas' heart and mind that day. But we do know that many people in desperate situations cry out to God before they ever know who He really is and how great His plan is for their lives. One of the Bible passages that affirms this is Psalm 107:13,14, "'Lord, help!' they cried in their trouble, and he saved them from their distress. He led them from the darkness and deepest gloom; he snapped their chains" (NLT).

I believe God looked down through the eons of time and saw Barabbas standing there, imprisoned for his deeds. Jesus loved Barabbas, and this political insurrectionist was the first person to be set free as Jesus took his place, willingly enduring the judgment that was due Barabbas.

How did this happen? It started with the demand of the crowd. Knowing he had the authority to set only one prisoner free, Pilate asked the unruly mass of people, "Who would you have me release, Jesus or Barabbas? The King of Kings or this political insurrectionist?"

The crowd shouted, "Give us Barabbas!"

Barabbas must have been shocked when he heard the choice offered to the crowd. Forced to decide between a convicted murderer or an innocent man who harmed no one and only went about doing good, the choice seemed obvious. Surely the crowd would choose Jesus! Many of the people in the crowd had most likely either seen Him performing miracles or had received one! But God had another plan - and Barabbas stands in stunned silence as the crowd cries for him to be freed and Jesus to be crucified! As we consider this scene, we should remember Romans 5:8, "But God showed his great love for us by sending Christ to die for us while we were still sinners" (NLT).

The powerful work of Jesus' redemption begins with Barabbas! The name Barabbas means, "son of the father," and Jesus was passionate about reaching him. He was fulfilling Isaiah 45:4, which says, "I

called you by name when you did not know me..."
(NLT).

There is a legend that has circulated through the years. It has not been verified, but is very interesting. The story is told that Barabbas and Judas were friends and had a common desire to overthrow their Roman oppressors. When Barabbas was arrested and condemned to death, Judas devised a plan he thought would be foolproof.

He would have Jesus arrested and brought before the authorities. Jesus would then be forced to reveal His power and authority ushering in His kingdom, freeing Himself, Barabbas and the Jewish people. However, Jesus declared that His kingdom was not of this world and Judas' plan backfired. Pilate releases Barabbas and Jesus is sent to be crucified. Judas, then overcome with grief, went out and hung himself.

We know that everything that happened that day was exactly as God had planned. The story goes on to say that after Barabbas was released, he followed Jesus all the way to Calvary. I am sure his life was never the same after being touched by Jesus' sacrifice. The most powerful thing to see is that Barabbas had nothing to do with his being set free. Jesus took his place, the innocent for the guilty.

Hundreds of years before the birth of Christ, Isaiah proclaims, "For a child is born to us, a son is given to us. And the government will rest on his shoulders. These will be his royal titles: Wonderful Counselor, Mighty God, Everlasting Father, Prince of Peace. His ever expanding, peaceful government will never end. He will rule forever with fairness and justice from the throne of his ancestor David. The passionate commitment of the Lord Almighty will guarantee this!" (Isaiah 9:6, NLT). There will never be peace without the Prince of Peace.

Barabbas' story speaks to us that the power of God and the reach of the cross need to affect government and politics. In God's heart is a passion to reach the governments of the nations. It is tragic that many in our nation do not want a vestige or remembrance of God's law in our courtrooms or in our statutes. We take symbols of the Ten Commandments out of our judicial buildings and allow injustice to reign within our courtrooms. We burn our flags and demean our leaders. There is a ferocious battle raging for the soul of America.

God has made Jesus the Lord over all kings and governmental leaders. Ephesians 1:21 says that God put Christ "far above any ruler or authority or power or leader or anything else in this world or in the world to come" (NLT). We used to sing, "Jesus, Jesus, there's just something about that Name...Kings and kingdoms will all pass away, but there's something about that Name" (*There's Just Something About That Name, Gaither Music Company*). The might of Rome, which once held the whole world in its fist, was destroyed - yet the kingdom of God remains. The power of Egypt, which once ruled the world was destroyed - but the kingdom of God remains. The power of the Persians, the power of the Babylonians - these great empires of the past are no more. Yet the kingdom of God remains.

In our generation we are seeing God move powerfully in the governments of nations. Think about what happened in the U.S.S.R. and how rapidly its Communist regime disintegrated. I grew up having to do air raid drills in school. We had to crawl under our desks to protect ourselves from a potential atomic bomb from the Russians. During the 1950s and 60s, schools had stockpiles of rations and water because we lived under the constant threat of attack. Yet in one day that mighty Soviet barrier, the Iron Curtain, came crashing down and the gospel went in. History is cluttered with the wreckage of nations that forgot God and died.

Christian analysts once said the gospel would never get into the 10/40 window, the Middle East, where civilization began. Now the gospel goes all around the world, including the 10/40 window. People from this region used to tell Christians, "Your God will never get in here! The great wall of Islam will never allow the gospel to be preached! We'll behead you and cut your tongue out!" Yet, through a series of events, there is now a tear in the fabric of Islam. For years, I have been hearing stories in which Jesus Himself has appeared to Muslims who are spiritually hungry, and they have given their lives to Christ in lands where no gospel witness was allowed to penetrate national borders.

Jesus rules the nations. The Bible says, "Why do the nations rage, and the people plot a vain thing? The kings of the earth set themselves, and the rulers take counsel together, against the Lord and against His Anointed, saying 'Let us break Their bonds in pieces and cast away Their cords from us'" (Psalm 2:1-3, NKJV). People want to cast off the chords of Christ, but God the Father declares to them that He has set His chosen King on the throne (see Psalm 2:6). God reigns securely and firmly. There is a passion in the heart of God to touch governments. The King is coming!

Godly rule does not happen without a biblical foundation. Political leaders may take the position that the church does not affect politics and politics does not affect the church. But that is wrong because the church has always been the voice of conscience to government. It has been the church throughout history that has risen up against social wrongs. From John the Baptist all the way down to the reformers who spoke out against slavery, the nonvoting status of women, and countless other social injustices, it has been the church that rose up and brought change in society.

America was founded upon Christian values. Patrick Henry declared: "It cannot be emphasized too strongly or too often that this great nation was founded, not by religionists, but by Christians, not on religions but on the gospel of Jesus Christ! For this very reason peoples of other faiths have been afforded asylum, prosperity, and freedom of worship here." (Steve C. Dawson, God's Providence in America's History, 1988).

Proverbs 14:34 teaches us, "Godliness exalts a nation, but sin is a disgrace to any people" (NLT). I am grateful when our country elects a president who gets on his knees and honors the living God. I thank

God when there is righteous movement in government to remove filth and perversion communicated through the media. If a godly ruler takes a stand against immorality, a person may complain, "Hey, you're taking away my rights!" But true freedom is not the right to do anything one chooses. A person may think he can do what he wants, but he does not realize that it costs him dearly when he attempts to obtain freedom apart from the Word of God. Wherever sin is liberalized in a society, there is more divorce, more child abuse, more immorality, and more fragmentation of people's hearts and lives. Righteousness exalts a nation. Sin is a shame to any people.

I am greatly encouraged by the words of Psalm 33:12, "Blessed is the nation whose God is the Lord" (NKJV). We all want to be blessed and we want our national government blessed. One way we can do that is to vote. If you are a Christian, I urge you to vote! You need to make a difference. All you have to do is watch the advertisements on TV that pander after the young generation. Our media and our educational institutes are filled with liberalism. Most kids do not know what they want and they cannot see the end results of bad decisions. So our society is capturing a generation, all the while the church sleeps. Exercise your right to vote, and then exercise your freedom in prayer!

It is interesting that the first person Jesus set free was a zealot politician. Jesus loved Barabbas so many years ago and He loves political leaders today. The church needs to reach out to our Barabbas (government leaders) with the loving passion of the Cross.

A few years ago the Lord prompted me to approach my local city government leaders and ask how we might be able to help them serve our city. I made an appointment with our mayor. During my first visit the mayor was taken aback and rushed me out of his office as quickly as possible. He had a difficult time believing I was not there to ask for some kind of favor or to complain about something.

The problem was that the church had been out of the government arena for so long we were strangers to them; they did not know how to take us. The Lord directed us to begin serving our city by doing block parties and neighborhood cleanups. We went into the very worst neighborhoods and began to minister to the people. We cleaned up empty lots, repaired houses, fed people, gave away clothing and shared the gospel.

After a few months of doing this type of ministry, I received a call from a city council member officially inviting me to speak at the inauguration for the mayor and newly elected city council members. I was thrilled! In twenty years of ministry that was the first such invitation I had ever received.

As I entered city hall that day my life and my relationship to our city government would change forever. I congratulated them on winning their seats and then I began to share with them what an overwhelming task they were faced with - the difficult times in which we live, increasing social woes, economic challenges and the constant threat of terrorism. I asked how many of them felt they needed help in their new position; they all raised their hands. I invited them to pray and ask for God's help and guidance to lead our city and they were excited to do it.

From that day forward my staff and I have been very involved in ministering to our city and have seen God do many wonderful things. What's interesting is that as we began to take this first step to entering the arena of government locally, God began to open doors for us to minister to government leaders at various levels of authority both nationally and internationally.

We must believe for the reach of the cross into government and politics. We must bring the love of God, the wisdom of God and the power of God back into the arena of government.

The Bible tells us ultimately every person will acknowledge God's rule and one day every person, from the most powerful to the insignificant will bow and confess that Jesus Christ is truly Lord of all. Psalm 72:11 says, "All kings will bow before him, and all nations will serve him" (NLT); Philippians 2:10-11 states, ". . . at the name of Jesus every knee should bow, of those in heaven, and of those on earth, and of those under the earth, and that every tongue should confess that Jesus Christ is Lord, to the glory of God the Father" (NLT).

Barabbas, the Lord is passionate about reaching you.

CHAPTER 4

SIMON OF CYRENE

THE CROSS REACHES INTO RACE RELATIONS

The next person Jesus impacted as He journeyed to Calvary was Simon of Cyrene, who represents Jesus' passion to reach all people and all races. Cyrene was in Africa, and Simon was more than likely a black man. A black man became the only person allowed to share the sufferings of Jesus on the way to Calvary. Think about it! Jesus first set free a politician; then in the plan and purpose of God, He chose a person from an ethnic group that was not His own to carry His cross.

Something happened to Simon as he shared the burden of carrying that cross with Jesus. Though he was forced into this suffering, and most likely his heart was filled with hatred for the Romans who oppressed him, the blood that was flowing from Jesus' wounds began to touch Simon and his life would forever change. The more Simon walked along under this incredible burden, the freer he became! This reminds me of the words that Peter, who was also present during Jesus' crucifixion, would later write: "For you know that God paid a ransom to save you from the empty life you inherited from your ancestors. And the ransom he paid was not mere gold or silver. He paid for you with the precious lifeblood of Christ, the sinless, spotless Lamb of God" (1 Peter 1:18, 19, NLT).

Many scholars believe that Simon later became a Christian. Some believe that he is the same Simon in Acts 13:1 which reads: Among the prophets and teachers of the church at Antioch of Syria were Barnabas, Simeon (called "the black man"), Lucius (from Cyrene), Manaen (the childhood companion of

King Herod Antipas), and Saul" (NLT).

Mark specifically tells us in his gospel that Simon was the father of Alexander and Rufus (see Mark 15:21), and we wonder if the Rufus mentioned in Romans 16:13 is the son of this Simon: "Greet Rufus, whom the Lord picked out to be his very own; and also his dear mother, who has been a mother to me" (Romans 16:13, NLT). From bitterness and suffering to freedom through the Cross!

It is the heart of God to reach all people, all nations, all races. Christianity is not a religion of people with a certain ethnic or cultural background. It is a relationship with God that is freely available to everyone. Simon represents more than a person of a different color. He presents a prophetic picture the Lord saw from the beginning of time showing that minorities and impoverished peoples would suffer at the hand of others who subjected them. This oppression is outside of His plan, and He feels the pain when one race is in cruel subjection to another.

It is important to realize that Simon was forced to carry the huge, heavy timbers that composed Jesus' cross. The King James Version of the Bible says that he was "compelled" to carry it (see Matthew 27:32). Simon did not willingly step up; he was compelled.

There are many forced issues in society, and people can be nasty to others who do not fit into their group. All throughout human history, there have been ethnic groups who unjustly dominate others, but we are reminded that Jesus is the Lord of all peoples and all nations. The cross sets people free! Revelation 5:9 expresses the true heart of God, "You [Jesus] were slain, and have redeemed us to God by Your blood out of every tribe and tongue and people and nation."

Jesus has a passion that His cross will reach every living person and that His wisdom will be made known to all. Ephesians 3:10 states God's purpose is that "the manifold wisdom of God might be made known by the church to the principalities and powers in the heavenly places." The word manifold in the Greek means "multifaceted; multicolored." The New Living Translation uses these words in Ephesians 3:10: "...wisdom in all its rich variety." God wants the church to display His wisdom and to tear down the principalities and powers that have put divisions among His people. The church needs to display the manifold wisdom of God, and that means to change the atmosphere of prejudice that divides us.

Prejudice is very often a spiritual thing. I believe principalities and powers incite hatred among ethnic groups, which is then perpetuated from generation to generation. The Lord did not forget oppressed people, hurt people, broken people or rejected people. He said, "Listen, there is a place at My cross for you." Finding identity in your life comes through acceptance and forgiveness - it is never found in rejection. No matter what the world hands you, no matter how much pain you go through, there is a God who loves you, and there is a place where significance can be found in your life if you embrace the cross instead of rejection and hatred.

Jesus boldly declared that God's love and redemption reaches to the whole world, to all people. We read in John 3:16, "For God so loved the world that He gave His only begotten Son, that whoever believes in Him should not perish but have everlasting life." This - the fact that God would offer salvation to all people - was revolutionary!

The early church in the book of Acts had to face the challenges to minister cross culturally. Jesus said in Acts 1:8, "But you shall receive power when the Holy Spirit has come upon you; and you shall be witnesses to Me in Jerusalem, and in all Judea and Samaria, and to the end of the earth."

The gospel had to be taken across the barriers that had separated peoples, tribes and nations. Step by step, guided by the Holy Spirit, the early disciples carried Jesus' message of forgiveness and redemption to the whole world.

A multicultural, multicolored, multifaceted church becomes a spear in the side of the principalities and powers, and when that happens, the church can break down the whole structure and system of prejudice.

I know there are many churches God is using powerfully today to overcome this spirit of racism. One of the many is Shiloh Christian Fellowship in Oakland, California. Shiloh is pastored by two very dear friends of mine, David and Marilyn Kiteley. The church was started more than forty years ago by David's mother, Violet Kiteley in 1965. Oakland was and still is a very tough city. It has had more than its share of racial problems. Shiloh has been highly effective in breaking the spirit of racism and building one of the most wonderfully diverse churches in America. People from over fifty different nations attend Shiloh. I have ministered there many times and have so enjoyed the wonderful atmosphere of acceptance and love for all.

My wife asked me a question after we had ministered there. She said, "Why do I feel so at home, so comfortable, so genuinely loved by so many diverse people in Shiloh?" She continued, "It doesn't matter who the people are, African Americans or Asians or Hispanics, I feel the same. I never feel any racial tension. I feel at ease, no walking on egg shells. I am just comfortable being true brothers and sisters in the Lord."

I thought about what made this church so special and I felt like the Lord dropped something into my heart. I responded, "It's because they have their priorities straight. They are Christians first and African-Americans second; they are Christians first and Asians second; they are Christians first and Hispanics second; they are Christians first and rich or poor second." That may sound simplistic, but it makes all the difference in the world in overcoming racism and prejudice. We are Christians first! Racism seeks to divide us by magnifying our differences, but when we accept Christ His blood makes us one body, one family, one church!

That sounds wonderful, but what practical steps can be taken to overcome racism? Pastor David Kiteley shares pearls of wisdom he has learned through the years.

"We were intentional and deliberate in targeting specific groups of people. From the very inception of Shiloh, people have driven from all over the Bay Area

to attend the church. This has created an exception-
ally diverse congregation. We believed that we had
a directive from God to produce a church that was
a picture of the composition of heaven as seen in
Revelation 7:9. We did not believe that this would
happen by accident, but it had to be purposeful by
design. We intentionally hired ministers from different ethnic, gender, generational and economic backgrounds. The vision of diversity must be done with a
high degree of sincerity and birthed out of love and
a concern for the people, and not some popularized
fad.

"A few years ago, the Barna Research Group
conducted a survey that found more than 92% of
the congregations in America were compromised of
at least 89% one racial group. The face of America
is rapidly changing today as the demographics of the
city, suburbs and rural areas shift. Our county is one
of the most diverse counties in the nation. In the
city of Oakland, over 70 languages are spoken. The
workplace, schools, malls and fast food restaurants
have kept up with the changing multiethnic society.
If the church is going to survive and grow in the 21st
Century, we must be relevant and address those God
has put in our communities. The only way that this
can happen is to boldly confront the two giants of

racism and sectarianism. Dr. Martin Luther King said, 'The most segregated hour is from 11-12 on Sunday mornings.' There is a price to pay for embracing a multicultural vision. It has not always been welcomed by the other segments of the church.

"We believe that the Civil Rights Movement was birthed by the Lord, therefore we participated in many demonstrations, including civil rights marches, in the city. We strongly believe the inequities and injustices of prejudices that gave rise to racial and denominational division grieve the bosom heart of God, and needed to be eradicated from the wounded, fractured, Body of Christ.

"Following are some of the principles which have made Shiloh an effective multicultural church:

1) Racial reconciliation must be considered a mandate from God rather than a politically correct popularized fad.

2) Intentionality - A multicultural church does not come into existence by accident. At the top of the intentionality list are deliberately hiring pastors and leaders from different ethnic backgrounds, and deliberately appointing members of different backgrounds to ministry positions.

3) Care for the multiethnic community in the

city – We discovered that as commendable as it was for Shiloh to have an extraordinary concern for our members of different ethnic backgrounds, it was not enough. We also needed to develop a compassion for the multiethnic community around them.

4) Cross cultural fellowship – Coming together to worship on Sunday at the Communion Table without eating together and sharing at the supper table does not reflect a true sense of love and harmony and unity that Jesus intended for His body to engage in.

5) Diversity in music and the arts - The church needs to have diversity in music and the arts in order to express the rich diversity that God has deposited in the various cultures. If you teach people to enlarge their spiritual appetite and repertoire, their taste buds can handle a diversity of worship styles and uniqueness of response. I think some of that is becoming easier during the renewal; many people are becoming outwardly expressive. However, if people are locked into one kind of music and worship form, they get uncomfortable at times. That is primarily why the church divided at Azusa Street. We are beginning to see some hopeful signs of reunification taking place with many of the celebrations which are transpiring in Southern California in 2006 in recognition of the Azusa Revival Centennial.

6) Multicultural churches provide opportunities for practical education. We discovered that it was vital that we communicate and learn from people of diverse cultures and backgrounds. As we listened to their history, struggles and the journey they have taken through life, we became aware of our common humanity. We began receiving people as individuals and started appreciating the unique giftings and contributions which they give to our lives and, in turn, we can reciprocate back to them.

7) Multicultural churches treat people with fairness, respect and consistency. It is vital that everyone feel their contribution and their concerns will be heard; there is no special preference given to any group, and the policies apply to everybody. In matters of discipline or correction, everyone is on equal playing ground and must be under the standards of the Word of God. Decisions are not made arbitrarily.

"The diversity in Shiloh has been the result of a mandate from the Lord. It is a supernatural move of God that does not just flow of good will or some passing fad. This supernatural move contains DNA we have been blessed to see imparted in many national and international outgrowths of Shiloh. Many other congregations and para-church groups which were birthed out of Shiloh possess this same mandate for multiethnic reconciliation and are experiencing similar results."

(Excerpts from Forty Years of Increase: The Shiloh Miracle, author: David R. Kiteley)

My prayer for our congregation, and for all of God's people, is that we grow to become more and more color blind. We want people from all races and all places, red and yellow, black and white - we are all precious in His sight.

Jesus is passionate about reaching people of all kinds. God wants us to be gathered together in His love from every tribe, every kingdom, every nation and every tongue.

CHAPTER 5

JOSEPH OF ARIMATHEA:
THE CROSS REACHES INTO BUSINESS AND FINANCE

Joseph of Arimathea, the wealthy man who provided a tomb for the body of Jesus, represents the reach of the cross into business and finance. The Bible characterizes Joseph as an honorable man who was waiting for the kingdom of God, but was a secret follower of Jesus: "Afterward Joseph of Arimathea, who had been a secret disciple of Jesus (because he feared the Jewish leaders), asked Pilate for permission to take Jesus' body down" (John 19:38, NLT; see also Mark 15:43). Joseph gathered his courage, went to Pilate, the ruler of the whole region of Judah, and asked for Jesus' body. Joseph's request was granted, and he wrapped the body of Jesus in linen and put it in his rock-hewn tomb.

The Lord is reaching for business people, and one of the arenas of society the church must take back is the area of business and commerce. It is important to realize that Joseph was secretly waiting for the kingdom of God and watching Jesus' life. Joseph never came out and told people who he was, but when he saw the crucifixion, something transformed him and changed his relationship to Jesus and the kingdom of God.

Joseph was deeply moved as he saw Jesus' crucifixion and death. This "secret disciple" decided it was time to boldly step forward and use his resources and influence to minister to the body of Christ. Joseph was not alone, Nicodemus joined him. They were both members of the Sanhedrin (Jewish Council) and they were both very influential.

John's gospel account tells Joseph's story this way:

"Afterward Joseph of Arimathea, who had been a secret disciple of Jesus (because he feared the Jewish leaders), asked Pilate for permission to take Jesus' body down. When Pilate gave him permission, he came and took the body away. Nicodemus, the man who had come to Jesus at night, also came, bringing about seventy-five pounds of embalming ointment made from myrrh and aloes. Together they wrapped Jesus' body in a long linen cloth with the spices, as is the Jewish custom of burial. The place of crucifixion was near a garden, where there was a new tomb, never used before. And so, because it was the day of preparation before the Passover and since the tomb was close at hand, they laid Jesus there" (John 19:38-42, NLT).

These two men had played it safe to this point, not willing to risk their reputation or jeopardize their "careers." They were curious about Jesus, but not willing to make a commitment. Unger's Bible Dictionary states that Nicodemus was one of the three wealthiest men in Jerusalem! I am sure that these men wanted to guard their status in the community, and they knew that aligning themselves with someone as radical as

Jesus would affect their social standing.

But suddenly, their perspective changed! They did not care what it cost them personally. They saw the sacrifice of Jesus; the reality of His message finally gripped their hearts and they were smitten. A deep desire began to stir in them, an urgency to minister to Jesus. What could they do? How could they serve Him?

They did not simply give enough to meet the need; they went way beyond. They gave in a manner that reflected their wealth.

Nicodemus brought enough embalming material (75-100 pounds) to prepare well over 200 bodies, according to Adam Clarke's commentary. This was a very lavish gift. Large amounts of embalming spices were used like this to show respect for royalty. Nicodemus presented a gift worthy of the King of Kings!

Joseph and Nicodemus worked together combining their resources and influence to minister to Jesus. Joseph gave Jesus his own tomb. Our faith in Jesus makes us generous, according to Philemon 6: "You are generous because of your faith. And I am praying that you will really put your generosity to work, for in so doing you will come to an understanding of all the good things we can do for Christ" (NLT).

I wonder if we have ever considered how significant the actions of Joseph and Nicodemus were that day. Do you know where bodies of crucified criminals were sent? Let me tell you where Jesus' discarded body would have ended up if Joseph had not intervened. Condemned criminals' bodies were usually left on their crosses to be ravaged by wild animals or thrown in a place called Gehenna, a trash heap outside of town. Fires burned continually in Gehenna. The townspeople threw dead dogs there; they threw garbage there; and they threw the carcasses of condemned criminals there. All the disciples had fled into hiding and no one had taken responsibility for burying Jesus' body! But Isaiah had prophesied more than 700 years earlier that Jesus would make His bed in death with the rich (see Isaiah 53:9). There was a prophetic destiny that one day a businessman would rise up and minister to the body of Christ so it would not be thrown into the ash heap.

Can you imagine how awful it would have been for the precious body of the Son of God to be thrown into the trash to be burned like a dog? Have you ever wondered how we would have known that Jesus rose from the dead? Who would have noticed that His body was missing from a garbage heap? Thank God, Joseph stepped up to bury Jesus in his tomb so angels could later announce from its entrance, "He is not here, but is risen!"

Think about Joseph and ask yourself who had the influence to go to Pilate, the ruler of Judah? Who had access into the halls of government? Who had right of entry into the highest levels of power? Joseph did, and Joseph kept his faith a secret until it was time for him to rise up.

I believe God is raising up a "Joseph Company" today. The church is going to experience a Joseph anointing similar to the anointing that came upon the first Joseph in Egypt (see Genesis 41:41-43). We are going to rule Egypt like Joseph did. There is an anointing, the reach of the cross into business, by which God is going to raise up godly men and women in areas of business and commerce. They will have a passion to minister to the body of Christ. They are going to lift the body of Christ from the ash heap and put it back into a place of prominence. We are going to break that spirit of poverty.

It is important to realize that real success is not just about having money. There are so-called "successful" people with all kinds of money who are living empty meaningless lives. Money does not equal success. Serving God is success. Having purpose for your life is success. Proverbs says, "The whole city celebrates when the godly succeed...Upright citizens bless a city and make it prosper, but the talk of the wicked tears it apart" (Proverbs 11:10, 11, NLT).

I believe one key to success in our businesses and in our communities is taking care of the poor. The Bible gives many promises to those who give to the less fortunate. Didn't Jesus say when we bless people who seem to be the least important we are blessing Him? When we feed the poor, clothe the naked and visit people in prison, we are doing it as unto Him. Jesus says, "I assure you, when you did it to one of the least of these my brothers and sisters, you were doing it to me!" (Matthew 25:40, NLT).

God is raising up people with a Joseph anointing who see the body of Christ and realize their true purpose; people of influence who can go into government, and when they speak, government is going to listen. God is after "holy Joes." He is calling holy Josephs who will go to the Pilates, go to the governors, go to the mayors and even go to presidents and say, "Let go of the body of Christ. Release the body of Christ and let it rise to a place of honor."

Through the years I have seen many wonderful ministries that have needed help at times from a "Joseph." They needed someone who would use his or her finances or influence at a key moment to help them break through, but the Josephs stayed in the shadows, not willing to risk or help. I have also seen some "Josephs" step forward at the proper time, and miracles take place.

One such miracle occurred when Mt. Zion Ministries started our compassion ministry. In the mid to late 1990s our city of Utica, New York was in tremendous economic upheaval. We suffered a major loss of jobs and many people began to be in need. Local food banks were inundated with needy people and soon ran out of both food and grant money. A local college did a study on poverty and the newspaper collaborated with them to do a series of articles on the growing crisis. As I read the statistics and saw most of our food pantries were running completely out of food and money halfway through the year, the Lord spoke to my heart to get a large warehouse, fill it with food and feed every hungry person in Utica! I began to look for a building and after a few months found a 30,000 square foot warehouse. The asking price was $400,000! This was far beyond anything we could afford, but the building was perfect for our needs.

I called a realtor and asked to see the building. As she went to put the key in the door she winced in pain and asked if I would open the door for her. Noticing her pain, I offered to pray for her. As I did, she was deeply touched and began to cry. She then told me that her future husband owned this building and he was very wealthy. She said he might want to help us with this wonderful ministry we were starting. In a matter of minutes I found myself in the office of one of the wealthiest men in our city. The realtor made the introductions and tried to explain as best she could what we wanted to do to help the poor. He quickly said he wanted to help us and he would sell us the building for $200,000, offering to hold the mortgage and work out any type of payment we could afford. I asked if he would give me a week to pray about it and get back to him. He agreed.

As I went to prayer, the Lord spoke to me to ask him to donate the building to us for free! I was very skeptical, considering this man was not a believer! I called the realtor and told her we wanted to ask him to donate the building. She said he had already donated quite a bit of money to the local college, hospital, community foundation and other organizations and he probably would not want to donate anything else. I said, "Tell him the Bible says whoever gives to the poor lends to the Lord and he will reward them for what they do." She left, not leaving me with much hope.

I did not hear a word from anyone for about three months! One day as I was going through my mail I opened a letter from this businessman's company stating that if I still wanted the building, he would donate it to us for one dollar! What a miracle! Our "Joseph" stepped forward in a crisis moment and made a way for us to start a wonderful ministry that has literally blessed multiplied thousands! Last year alone, just in our local area, we gave away 250,000 boxes of food! We also ship numerous containers overseas to other nations. We have begun a children's feeding program, in the first year alone serving over 1,000 children a week. From the act of one Joseph, multitudes have been blessed!

It is time for the Josephs to come out of the shadows and step up. These people must rise up and take the body of Christ off the ash heap and begin to lift it to prominence. The kingdom of God must come to our communities.

Joseph of Arimathea risked it all. He risked his

reputation, his life, and he went to the "powers that be" and said, "Let go of the body of Christ." He used his influence to extend the kingdom, and we need to do the same.

CHAPTER 6

THE CRUCIFIED CRIMINALS:

THE CROSS REACHES INTO SOCIAL PROBLEMS

According to Luke 23:39-43, "One of the criminals hanging beside Christ scoffed, 'So you're the Messiah, are you? Prove it by saving yourself - and us, too, while you're at it!' But the other criminal protested, 'Don't you fear God even when you are dying? We deserve to die for our evil deeds, but this man hasn't done anything wrong.' Then he said, 'Jesus, remember me when you come into your Kingdom." And Jesus replied, 'I assure you, today you will be with me in paradise'" (NLT).

Jesus was crucified between two criminals, one on His left and one on His right. I am sure you have seen artwork depicting that scene with the three crosses - two condemned criminals with Jesus crucified between them. At first, they both mocked Him along with the crowd, but as time went by one of the criminals began to change.

This passage of Scripture is a graphic picture of people trapped in the cycle of deception. These men were condemned because of what they had done; they were tried and found guilty. One man recognizes his sin and acknowledges Jesus as Savior. The other sees Jesus only as a way to escape his present troubles, demanding, "If you are God then get me out of this mess!"

The thief who asked Jesus to help him escape his situation reminds me of two other thieves who tried to shift blame in the Garden of Eden. Adam and Eve plucked fruit off a tree they were not supposed to touch.

God came and asked, "Adam, what did you do?"

Adam replied, "Me? I didn't do anything."

Pointing to Eve, Adam accused her: "She did it. Everything was cool until she showed up. It's not my fault."

Next God turned to the woman and asked, "What have you done?"

Her excuse: "Me? It wasn't my fault. I've only been here a short while. I thought I'd share with Adam. It was the serpent."

This narrative from the third chapter of Genesis is indicative of our tendency to shift blame. We think, "It's not my fault, it's not my responsibility, I didn't do it."

Proverbs 19:3 tells us "People ruin their lives by their own foolishness and then are angry at the Lord" (NLT). I have observed many people through the years as they have ruined their lives, their marriages, their families and their careers through continual sin. Instead of acknowledging their wrong and seeking forgiveness, they looked for someone or something to blame, sometimes even God! Blaming someone or something else is a huge problem in our culture today. Just try to get someone to admit they were wrong. Try to get someone to say, "I did it, I'm the person, I'm sorry." It is a rare occurrence when someone actually accepts responsibility for wrongdoing.

Another problem in our society is the practice of seeking to re-label or redefine everything. We want to redefine family, sin, morality, even God. The further we move from the absolute truth of God's Word, the more confusing life becomes. People are deceived to want to follow a "new path" of enlightenment and move beyond the "archaic" principles of the Bible.

Jeremiah 6:16-17 warns us, "Yet the Lord pleads with you still: 'Ask where the good road is, the godly paths you used to walk in, in the days of long ago. Travel there, and you will find rest for your souls.' But you reply, 'No, that is not the road we want!' I set watchmen over you who warned you: 'Listen for the sound of the trumpet! It will let you know when trouble comes.' But you said, 'No! We won't pay any attention!'" (TLB).

We must pay attention and heed God's warnings; we must turn back to Him and confess our sins. Proverbs 29:1 warns us, "If you keep being stubborn after many warnings, you will suddenly discover you have gone too far" (CEV).

I encourage you: do not be a blame shifter, do not blame past generations as an excuse or try to re-label sin. Do not shrug off responsibility by saying, "It's not my fault." Take personal responsibility; acknowledge your sin to God; ask to be forgiven and healed by the reach of the cross.

The cross is the answer for addiction, and what an addicted society we are. There is a better way to deal with our problems than by masking our pain with drugs or alcohol. Too easily we crave false "cures" we hear advertised on television: "Are you depressed? Feeling a bit blue? Is your child hyperactive? Just get our product and everything will be alright!" We miss the fact that when we unthinkingly grab for a "magic pill" instead of reaching for the cross, we can become psychological hypochondriacs. When we thought-lessly reach for fast "cures" instead of reaching to the cross, we miss the truth that what our children really need is discipline, good parenting, normalcy, and love from the house of God. Healing, freedom from addictions, real love and forgiveness, all things our society is searching for, are found at the cross.

Judy Pucillo, a great friend and minister in our church, shares the following true life story of how Christ reached into her life - dramatically freeing her from a lifetime of abuse, hatred, pain and addiction. Without a doubt, she would not be alive today had she not been impacted by the reach of the cross. Here is her story:

I was born and raised in Brooklyn, New York and brought up in a Christian home. My mother attended a small Hispanic Pentecostal Church where she would often bring my sister and me. As a young child, I knew about Jesus and how He loved the little children.

My family was not wealthy, but I was content, a happy little girl until I was six years old. From that time on the sparkle in my eyes left. I was sexually abused at that age and it continued throughout all of my childhood and into my early twenties. Family members, neighbors, strangers all came and went.

Abusers never take responsibility for their actions; they impart guilt, shame and fear. I was stripped of my identity and femininity. I had no say because I was controlled by threats. I began to believe what I was told; that I was a naughty little girl; that I was evil and no good and if I were to tell my parents, they would throw me out of the house because they didn't love me anyway.

I remember that very first night lying there in pain and full of fear. With tears running down my cheeks I heard a voice telling me, "Now Jesus loves the little children, but does He really love you? He didn't protect you now did He?" That was the first seed of rejection that was planted in my life.

As the years went by, I became rebellious. I performed excellently in school, but because I had no peace or joy, I turned to drugs to escape reality and numb the pain. I experimented with pot, beer and pills. Then, I went deeper with cocaine, heroine and alcohol. From that time on, my life went downhill. I became a drug addict doing whatever I had to do to get a bag of dope. I was so strung out on drugs, I mentally blocked my childhood.

Thank God for a praying mom. My mother is a warrior. I know that it's because of her prayers that I'm alive and here today! I also thank my mom for the decision she had to make when she threw me out of the house because of my addiction. It snapped me out of denial and made me take responsibility and realize I needed help. No where to go, I ended up at my sister's house. Hitting rock bottom, I began to have suicidal thoughts. It was then one night, in my sister's bathroom, I picked up a razor to kill myself. I heard a voice tell me, "Go ahead - do it. You've caused so much hurt and shame to everyone; they're better off without you!" Then I heard another voice, "I love you! Give me a chance!"

Eventually after hearing these voices, I threw the razor into the sink and fell on my knees committing my life to the Lord. I then asked Him for a sign. If He was real, I asked that when I got up the next morning, no matter how sick I was, that I would not go to the methadone clinic. Not only did I not leave my sister's house that day, but the Lord broke the chains of addiction and took away the desire to get high and hang out with the old crowd.

Soon, I met a wonderful man who had graduated from the Teen Challenge program. He treated me like a lady, totally different from anything I'd ever experienced. We dated and six months later got married. Because I no longer was using drugs, no longer escaping reality and numbing the pain, three weeks after my marriage, I began to relive my past which led to a nervous breakdown. For the first sixteen years of my marriage, I had three nervous breakdowns. I was in mental institutions with severe depression, was suicidal and on many prescriptions. I lived for years in the prison of my own home unable to leave for fear of being raped.

I thank God that I had a great husband who never gave up on me. He stood by me and kept on praying. I used to wonder why he loved me so much. I had a beautiful daughter too. That also was a miracle because supposedly I couldn't have any children, yet God gave her to me. Still, in August of 1994, I felt so worthless as a wife and mother that I planned to kill myself. But God's hand and mercy were upon my life.

To see total healing and restoration, I had to make one of the hardest decisions ever and that was to forgive everyone who had abused me. I was full of hatred, bitterness, rage, and unforgiveness. I used to fantasize how I would torture those that hurt me. I was living in a dream world to fulfill all this hatred, but one morning the Holy Spirit began to talk to me. In order to recover and truly be happy and experience peace, I would have to let go of the hatred, bitterness and unforgiveness. I had to forgive. Believe me - this was not easy, but I chose to forgive. It wasn't a feeling; it was a decision that I had to make and I did. Right then and there something broke. I felt lighter. I can't really explain it, but I knew I was on the right track.

What I forgot to do was to forgive myself. The process is not complete unless that happens. Emotions are difficult to handle. We may forgive, but that doesn't mean everything is forgotten right away.

It takes time for our emotions and our spirits to heal. Right thinking patterns needed to be developed.

God is so faithful. All through that week I tried to kill myself, every time I was going to attempt suicide, my husband, Charlie, or my daughter, Janelle, would come home. On a Thursday afternoon I remember saying, "God I need a miracle. Tomorrow even if they're here, I'm going to do it. I've already written the note; I've got it all planned out. Jesus, please help me. You know I mean it!"

That night my husband and I attended church. Nobody had any idea what I was going through. I was so overwhelmed by fear, hopelessness, and loneliness that even physically I felt cold. I knew I was close to death. When the service finished, I heard a woman saying that there was a healing service going on, a tent meeting in Rome, NY. I immediately asked my husband to take me, but he shrugged his shoulders and said he was tired. A gentleman stopped him at the doorway and asked him if he could give him a ride to Rome because he didn't have his bike with him; my husband said he couldn't and we went home. Just when I was about to get out of the car, he stopped me and felt convicted. We turned around and found the gentleman walking on the road toward Rome. It so happened that he wasn't going to his house; he was going to the healing service.

Tears welled up in my eyes. I got excited inside, but I quickly repressed it, just in case nothing really happened. When we got there, I noticed everyone had their hands up worshipping the Lord and singing, "Alleluia." It was very crowded. At the back of the tent, I paced like a lion in a cage. I always carried my "Brooklyn" pocketbook - everything was in it, including all the prescriptions. I gave it to my husband and literally pressed through the crowd.

I was met by a woman who also attended the same church as I. She asked me if I wanted prayer and I said, "Yes." By then, I was sobbing. She took me up front where I met two men from Virginia Beach who were holding the meetings. While one continued to play the organ, the other stopped singing and came to me. The service continued; everyone was still singing. I began to tell him what I intended to do. All I remember is his hand. I've never been slain by the Holy Spirit, and it felt like I was floating on a cloud. Such peace! My husband said I was there for 1 1/2 hours. I began to cry aloud, literally scream. I felt so much pain, and then I began to laugh. It was a genuine laughter. Just before I got up, I saw a little girl skipping in a garden with a daisy. Now, let me tell you - I'm from the ghetto, but I knew that that was me. When I came to, the weight of suicide left, fear left and I felt peace and joy. The Lord totally set me free.

The next day for the first time in years, my husband and I worshipped together and thanked the Lord for what He did. We have never been the same again. Now with the same comfort that the Lord has given me, I give to others. I know this for a fact - our past does not dictate our future. Nothing is impossible for God. I believe in miracles because I am one. I give Jesus Christ all the glory, honor and praise!!

Isn't that a powerful testimony? We are literally surrounded by people, just like Judy, who need the continual reach of the cross in their lives. David understood this, as we can see from his words in Psalm 32:1-6,

"What happiness for those whose guilt has been forgiven! What joys when sins are covered over! What relief for those who have confessed their sins and God has cleared their record. There was a time when I wouldn't admit what a sinner I was. But my dishonesty made me miserable and filled my days with frustration. All day and all night your hand was heavy on me. My strength evaporated like water on a sunny day until I finally admitted all my sins to you and stopped trying to hide them. I said to myself, 'I will confess them to the Lord.' And you forgave me! All my guilt is gone. Now I say that each believer should confess his sins to God when he is aware of them, while there is time to be forgiven. Judgment will not touch him if he does." (TLB)

Why don't you stop right now and ask yourself, "How do I look at the cross?"

CHAPTER 7

THE CENTURION:

THE CROSS REACHES INTO SPIRITUAL WARFARE FOR SOULS

The Roman centurion represents Jesus' heart - a passion to reach souls who are unknowingly trapped in spiritual warfare. Two kingdoms are in violent conflict - the kingdom of God and the kingdom of darkness. The Roman centurion was a military leader who had charge of one hundred soldiers. The sight of torture, maiming and killing was all too familiar to these battle-hardened veterans. As they crucified Jesus, they were not moved in the least.

How powerful the cross that it can reach the hardest of hearts!

At the cross Roman soldiers brutalized Jesus, yet all the while He was pleading, "Father, forgive them, for they do not know what they do" (Luke 23:34). The reach of the cross into the warfare for our souls is explained in Colossians 1:13, 14, "For he has rescued us from the one who rules in the kingdom of darkness, and he has brought us into the Kingdom of his dear Son. God has purchased our freedom with His blood and has forgiven all our sins" (NLT). Thank God! He reached into the darkness. He waged war with the one who held you; set you free and brought you into a kingdom where you would experience kindness and love.

What happened that day at Calvary? What was the scene the centurion witnessed? Matthew 27:45 tells us, "At noon, darkness fell across the whole land until three o'clock" (NLT). Not only did the midday sky turn black, the ground shook.

Matthew 27:54 records the centurion's reaction: "So when the centurion and those with him, who were guarding Jesus, saw the earthquake and the things that had happened, they feared greatly, saying, 'Truly this was the Son of God!'"

What would terrify a band of rough, tough warriors like this Roman centurion and his men? Can you imagine the sky at noon suddenly becoming pitch black and staying that way for three hours? Many thought it was the end of the world.

Let me ask you: Have you ever been any place where you sensed the icy chill of evil? You knew something dreadful was surrounding you as you felt the darkness, the fear and the depression of it. The Roman centurion shook to the core when darkness covered the earth for the three hours Jesus was on the cross. What was that darkness? I believe it was the sin of the entire world. The Bible says Jesus is the Lamb of God who takes away the sins of the world, and as Jesus died, the Roman centurion cried out, "Truly this Man was the Son of God!" (Mark 15:39, NLT).

Throughout the years before Christ - whether it was Adam's sin, Abraham's lying, Noah's drunkenness, the sins of the children of Israel who were led out of Egypt, David's adultery, all murders and incest - everyone's sin was put forward. It was being stored somewhere. (I don't know where God stores sin; I know sin isn't just erased!) Then at the cross God said, "This is the time. Here is the Suffering Servant, the Lamb of God. Go and get all the sins from the beginning of time and bring them here to this place called Calvary." All the sins from Adam forward, everything wrong that had ever been done, was brought and placed on Him. It began to get darker and darker.

Then God said, "Now, go into eternity-future (you've already got eternity-past) and bring Me all the sins that ever will be committed. Bring Me the sins of those here today, the sins of their children and the sins of those who are not even born yet. Go all the way to the end of time in the future, because no one can be exempted, and bring all their sins here to the cross of Calvary."

If God can bring sin from the beginning of time, God can reach to the end of time. All our sins were brought to this place called Calvary and for three hours they accumulated. Isaiah 44:22 says, "I have blotted out, like a thick cloud, your transgressions, and like a cloud, your sins. Return to Me, for I have redeemed you." Jesus reached out from the cross and cried, "It is finished!" And when the Roman centurion saw all that had happened, He praised God, saying, "Truly this Man was the Son of God!" The darkness was broken and light began to shine again. The cross of Jesus Christ triumphed in this soldier's life and made victory available to all who would believe.

CHAPTER 8

THE REACH OF THE CROSS FOR YOU

Let me give you a brief biblical overview to explain why the reach of the cross has the power to meet your deepest needs. When Adam and Eve sinned, God permanently expelled them from the garden. He told them they could not return because if they ate the Tree of Life in their sin, they would remain in a state of death forever. For this reason He barricaded the way to the Tree of Life by placing two angels with flaming swords to guard it. Engraved in Adam and Eve's memory was the painful reality that they could never get back to eternal life. They had to live the rest of their lives outside of the garden, but they had hope that one day a Messiah, a Savior, would come.

Much later, God delivered the children of Israel from oppression in Egypt, and they became a great nation under Moses. God told them He wanted to dwell corporately with His people and instructed them to build Him a tabernacle. Moses built the tabernacle that included an outer court and an inner sanctum (the Holy of Holies), where the ark of God was kept. The ark was the symbol of the presence of God. A curtain hung between the holy place and the Holy of Holies. God instructed Moses to weave two angels with flaming swords into that curtain. Once a year, the high priest went into the Holy of Holies and sprinkled the blood on the mercy seat. In order to do that, he had to part those two angels, and he did it very fearfully! (You may know that the priest tied a rope around himself in case he died from being in the holy presence of the Lord. That way, someone could pull him out without risking his own life.) The priest would go between those two angels and sprinkle the blood on the mercy seat to atone for the sins of the people.

Centuries later, in the temple of Jesus' time, the curtain that was hung between the holy place and the Holy of Holies also had two angels with flaming swords woven into the fabric. When Jesus died, God ripped that curtain, starting at the top: "And the curtain in the Temple was torn in two, from top to bottom" (Mark 15:38, NLT).

Do you know what that picture symbolizes? The way of approach to God is now open! You will never be rejected if you come to God. Isaiah 1:18 says, "'Come now, let us reason together,' says the Lord. Though your sins are like scarlet, they shall be as white as snow; though they are red as crimson, they shall be like wool" (NIV). God says, "I want to reason with you." You may say, "God, my sins are like scarlet." But God's answer is that your sins will be white like wool. Wool is so white and pure!

The word scarlet means "double." Actually the Hebrew word for scarlet meant to be "doubly dipped" or "doubly dyed." Here's a practical illustration of how indelible "scarlet" is.

When I first started washing my own clothes (my wife got liberated), I threw in a red shirt with whites - my underwear, to be exact. When I finished the wash, I had pink underwear. I said to my wife, "I am not going to wear pink underwear. Is there any hope this underwear will ever be white again?" There was no hope for those whites! They were irretrievably pink. Once they were dyed pink, they stayed pink.

The Bible says our sins are not just dyed once; they are doubly dipped. It is one thing to do something that can be forgotten or forgiven; it is another thing to be so stained that we feel we can never change. We think our souls are so tainted that we are doubly dipped. We think we are so bad we are beyond reach. That is a lie! We are not beyond the reach of the cross. God says, "I want to reason with you. Though your sins are that deep and that stained, I can make you white as wool." The blood of Jesus Christ is the answer for our stained souls.

The cross also reaches to touch people who feel forgotten and forsaken. Look at Isaiah 49:14-16. Verse 14 records the cry of Zion, a picture of the church, "But Zion said, 'The Lord has forsaken me, the Lord has forgotten me'" (NIV). Have you ever asked the Lord if He's forgotten you? God answers you with a question, the same answer He gave Isaiah in the next verse, "Can a woman forget the baby at her breast and have no compassion on the child she has borne?" So God's answer is, "Don't you know the love of a parent?"

Many people in our society have twisted values regarding natural parental love. We need only to read the newspaper or watch television to hear horrible stories about parents abusing, neglecting or murdering their children. Our society advocates abortion, but preaches against the death penalty for violent criminals. We can kill an innocent baby, but then we let a violent criminal live. You may say, "Well, Lord, I have never known the love of a parent. My parents didn't love me; my wife left me; my husband left me. I've known nothing but rejection." But the promise to you is that even though your mother may forget you (which is pretty hard for her to do, according to Isaiah 49:15), God says, "I will not forget you! See, I have engraved you on the palms of my hands" (Isaiah 49:15, 16, NIV). He says He will never forget you and here's the proof: He has engraved you in the palms of His hands - the same palms that were nailed to the cross for you.

Think about it! When Jesus was crucified, He was brutally beaten. With His swollen face, His body torn to shreds by the whipping and the beating and the pummeling, He must have looked horrific. But when Jesus walked out of the tomb at His resurrection, He was beautiful again except for five wounds, five scars, which He kept. He chose to keep them. He chose to be eternally disfigured and scarred forever with two wounds in His hands, a wound in His side, and two wounds in His feet. I believe it is because He said, "I will not forget you! See, I have engraved you on the palms of my hands."

After you receive Jesus and get to heaven, you will see those nail-scarred hands when He reaches out to greet you. His eyes will meet your eyes, and His gaze will penetrate your heart when you see how much He really cares for you. He will look in your eyes with all-encompassing pure love, and your heart will begin to melt as you realize: He really, really, really loves me. You are going to be melted by love that you have only dreamed about.

When you see Jesus the thought is probably going to rise up in your mind: I could have done more. I should have been secure in God's love. I should have moved out in that love. I should have told others about that love. But remember that He loves you. You are not going to see Jesus approaching you with fire coming out of His eyes or a flaming sword coming out of His hands. Instead, He will extend to you a nail-scarred palm. He wants you to always remember the price He paid because He loves you.

If you are already a Christian, I encourage you to allow the passion of the cross to reach you. Realize that because of the cross, He has removed your deepest stains and that nothing can separate you from His great love. Act on your faith, begin to reach out and tell others about the love of Christ. Begin to believe God for people around you to find the Lord.

If you have never opened up your heart to Him, know He is reaching for you. See those nail-scarred hands that were pierced for you. The power of His reach is great because He loves you. Let's believe God for the power of the cross to reach into every area of your life and into every aspect of society. As it does, we will see lives transformed and the world changed.

ABOUT THE AUTHOR

Mike Servello is the senior pastor of Mt. Zion Ministries in Utica, New York, a church he has pastored for twenty five years. He is also the author of *God's Shield of Protection*.

Mike serves on the Apostolic Leadership Team of Ministers Fellowship International.

He is also the founder and CEO of Compassion Coalition, a ministry which feeds tens of thousands of people annually in the U.S. and around the world.

Mike and his wife, Barbara, have been married for 33 years. They have three adult children and three grandchildren, Matthew, Abigail and Giulia.

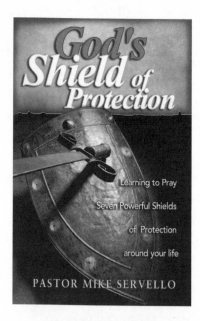

Create a hedge of God's protection around you and your family.

Wars. Terrorists. Disease. Tragedy and Devastation. In the midst of today's troubled times, we are all desperately searching for the Lord's peace and protection.

If we are to withstand Satan's attempts to destroy us and cripple us with fear, we have to learn to be pro-active in prayer concerning ourselves, our family, our friends, our nation and all that God has given us.

According to God's Word, it is possible through fervent, effectual prayer to live under Divine protection and to construct prayer hedges around your life and home that Satan cannot penetrate.

Inside *God's Shield of Protection,* you'll learn what rightly belongs to you as God's child, how to stay protected through intercession and how to build effective prayer hedges including: *Mental Hedges, Emotional Hedges, Physical Hedges, Spiritual Hedges, Moral Hedges, Financial Hedges, Ministerial Hedges.*

Prepare for every area of your life to be changed as you begin to integrate the principles found in this powerful book into your daily prayer life.